The
Sinister
Airfield

The Sinister Airfield

by Alison Prince

illustrated by Ellen Thompson

WILLIAM MORROW AND COMPANY
NEW YORK • 1983

Library of Congress Cataloging in Publication Data
Prince, Alison.   The sinister airfield.
Summary: After discovering a body in the woods adjacent to an unused airfield, three
children become suspicious that rustlers working in the area may be local peo-
ple.   [1. Robbers and outlaws—Fiction.   2. Mystery and detective stories]
I. Thompson, Ellen (Ellen M.), ill.   II. Title.   PZ7.P9358Si   1983
[Fic]   82-18877
ISBN 0-688-01741-X

For the many friends I have made in Suffolk,
a county whose landscapes of wide skies
suggested this book

Contents

The
Sinister
Airfield

Chapter 1
Warned Off

"Friday afternoon," said Ian. "Great! Two whole days with no school."

They were walking across the tarmac space in front of the school where the buses came.

"I don't really mind school," said Harrie. She glanced at the jostling lines of children waiting to get on the buses and added, "I'm glad we walk home, though. I'd hate to be squashed into a bus."

"You don't get *squashed*," Ian scoffed. "And just you wait until winter comes. You won't like walking home across the airfield then—not when it's cold and wet and dark."

"I walked home from the lower school," Harrie pointed out.

"Not half as far," said Ian. "And not across the airfield. It's creepy up there in the dark."

1

"I know," said Harrie crossly. She wished Ian wouldn't keep on about it. Secretly she dreaded the dark days to come. Even when the sun was shining, the airfield could be a frightening place, with its bleak emptiness and all those ruined buildings.

Ian glanced around and groaned. "Here comes trouble."

Harrie looked. A fat, beaming boy in glasses was approaching. "He doesn't look like trouble," she said.

"Stupid twit," said Ian. "He's in my class. Just moved here from London. Hello, Neil—what do *you* want?"

Neil beamed even more broadly. "Hope you don't mind," he said, "but I thought you might show me the way across the airfield. I live near you, but Mum said I wasn't to go poking around up there on my own. She thinks I'm going to fall down a quarry or something."

Harrie giggled because Neil had a funny squeaky voice, but he thought it was because of his mother's silly ideas.

"Daft, isn't it?" he agreed. "Dad's just as bad. But it's *miles* around by the road."

"Where do you live, then?" asked Harrie.

"Mill Gardens," said Neil. "The last house. I can

see right over the airfield from my bedroom and there's a footpath leads up there from the end of our road. So I thought if there was a shortcut, you'd know."

Mrs. Perritt, the crossing guard, had stopped the traffic. "Come on if you're coming!" she shouted. Ian and Harrie and Neil ran across. On the far side, where a rough dirt road led up to the airfield, Mutty was quietly waiting, his chin on his paws. He got to his feet as the children approached, yawned and stretched and waved his raggy tail.

"Hello, Mutty," said Harrie, patting him.

Neil eyed the dog doubtfully. "What sort is he?"

"Sheep dog crossed with wolfhound," said Ian.

"That's what Dad thinks, anyway," said Harrie. "It would explain him being so big and gray and shaggy, and the white chest and feet."

"What's he doing here?" asked Neil.

"Waiting," said Harrie simply. "He always comes to meet us, but he won't cross a road. So he waits here."

Neil skirted a pothole carefully. "It's a bit rough," he observed. "No good for cars. Is this the only way up to the airfield?"

"No, there's a turn off the main road," said Ian. "It goes up to the other side of the quarry, between here and your house. Trucks use it to cart the gravel away."

"This used to be a proper road in the war," said Harrie. "Dad says there were airplanes here then, and guns and things."

"And barbed wire all around," said Ian.

"Nothing but blackberries now," said Neil. "And nettles and those weedy looking bushes."

"They're elderberry," Harrie told him. She thought for a bit as they trudged on up the road, then added, "I wonder what it looked like in the war. When the buildings all had their roofs on and everything was neat and tidy. It's hard to imagine, the way it is now."

The road was climbing steeply between overgrown hedges, and Neil began to puff slightly.

"Going too fast for you?" asked Ian.

"Don't be so horrid, Ian," said Harrie, who had taken a liking to fat Neil with his squeaky voice.

"*Well!*" said Ian with contempt—and ran ahead with Mutty, leaping potholes energetically.

"He's awfully athletic," said Harrie apologetically. "He's always helped Dad on the farm, you see. He's not thirteen yet and he can carry a bale in each hand. *I* can't. But then, I'm only eleven."

"Fancy owning a farm," said Neil. "Aren't you lucky!"

Harrie laughed. "Oh, Dad doesn't *own* the farm!" she said. "He's the head cowman. The farm belongs to Mr. Ashworth. He owns the airfield, too."

Neil looked surprised. "What for? Does he fly airplanes?"

Harrie shook her head. "The runway's too far gone. Some airfields are used for crop-spraying aircraft, but the takeoff strip has to be nice and smooth. Not like this one."

They emerged from the narrow road onto the airfield itself. It was windswept and desolate, the concrete runway cracked and broken, blotched with thickets of blackberry. The afternoon sun was low on the horizon and shone red through the empty windows of the roofless brick buildings as though fires burned in them.

"It gives me the shivers a bit," said Harrie. "Some people say it's haunted by the ghosts of dead airmen. It's all right when the sun's shining the way it is now, but it'll be horrid in the winter when it's dark."

Neil nodded, gazing about him through the large, round glasses that gave him a popeyed look. "It's creepy," he agreed. "Perhaps it's because the aircrews must have felt all jittery, waiting for takeoff, and the scared feeling lives on after them."

"Or it's the spirits of the ones who were shot down," said Harrie. "Forever trying to come back with the others and take off their flying jackets."

"How awful," said Neil. "As if they were somehow condemned to be outside in the cold and the dark forever, while the others are singing songs and drinking cocoa, safe indoors."

They were walking past a ruined building, and as they neared the end a figure leaped out with a shriek, arms waving wildly. Harrie screamed, then shouted crossly, "Ian! You are a *beast!*"

Neil clutched at his heart in mock collapse as the grinning Ian fell in beside them. "Thought it was a ghost!" he gasped in his squeaky voice. Ian laughed, but without contempt this time. "Neil," he said, "do you like model aircraft?"

Neil nodded. "I've made heaps," he said. "They're all hanging up in my bedroom. Mum hates them. She says they gather dust."

"Radio control?" asked Ian.

"Don't be daft," said Neil. "Much too expensive."

"Lots of them up here on Saturday afternoons," Ian told him. "There's an airplane-modelers club meets here. You should see some of them. Terrific."

"Really?" Neil was excited. "Can we go?"

"Of course," said Ian casually. "My dad's a member."

"Where's Mutty?" interrupted Harrie, who found model aircraft boring.

"Gone ahead," said Ian. "We'll catch up in a minute."

Harrie looked anxious. "I hope he isn't in the wood," she said. "That new gamekeeper doesn't like dogs. Dad said we had to be careful." She quickened her pace.

"What d'you mean?" asked Neil, trotting a little to keep up with her.

"Gamekeepers shoot dogs sometimes if they think their pheasants are being disturbed. Old Cecil wouldn't have done it, but he retired last year."

"I don't like this new bloke," said Ian. "Always shouting at people."

They had reached the far side of the airfield. On their left a wooden fence marked the edge of a steep quarry, and Neil, peering over, saw huts and machinery a long way down. "Wouldn't like to fall down there," he said.

"You'd bounce." Ian grinned.

"I'm not *that* fat," Neil protested good-temper-edly. "But I'd be *flat* by the time I reached the bottom."

"Sure would," agreed Ian. "Hey—come and look at my calves."

He ran ahead to a gate that interrupted the hedge on their right, jumped up on it, and gave a piercing whistle. A group of black-and-white bullocks grazing some distance away pricked up their ears at the sound and ambled toward the gate.

"Those aren't calves," protested Neil. "They're blooming great cows!"

"Steers," corrected Ian. "Grand, aren't they? I helped Dad rear this lot. Best bunch we've had for a long time."

"What sort are they?" asked Neil.

"Friesians, of course!" snorted Ian.

Neil nodded cheerfully, uncrushed. "Don't know much about cows," he said.

"Oh, here's Mutty!" exclaimed Harrie, relieved as the big dog came bounding up. "Thank goodness! Let's not go through the wood, Ian."

"Don't be daft," said Ian firmly. "We've every right to go through the wood. If we go around by the quarry lane, we'll be back late."

"It doesn't matter," argued Harrie. "Dad can manage without you for a few minutes. And anyway, the quarry lane leads nearly all the way to Neil's house, so we can show him the best way to take tomorrow."

Ian shrugged. "Suit yourself," he said. Then an

idea struck him. "Neil—why not come back to our house? You'd like to see the farm, wouldn't you? And Dad's radio-controlled model?"

Harrie glared at her brother, but Neil beamed affably. "Great," he said. "As long as I can ring up my mum and tell her where I am. She worries."

"You can ring her when we get home," said Ian. "Come on—we'll go through the wood."

The lane curved away to the left, skirting around the quarry and becoming wider as it led steeply downhill. Ian stopped when they came to the wood and said, "To get to your house, Neil, just keep along the lane here and take the footpath that goes off to the right. You can see your house from there, across the sugar-beet field."

"Oh, yes," said Neil, nodding happily. "I know just where you mean. Thanks."

"This way's much quicker for us," said Ian.

Mutty had already trotted ahead of them into the wood, and Harrie followed him at a run. If they had to go through the beastly wood, it was better to do it quickly. She charged recklessly through the dry leaves, careless of noise. Birds flew up from the trees, clattering into the pink sky. Then she heard Mutty yelp.

She rushed around the next bend in the path— and stopped short. Right in front of her stood the gamekeeper, holding Mutty's collar in a twisted

grip, the dog dangling painfully from it, his front paws clear of the ground. The long twin barrels of a shotgun lying over the man's free arm glinted red in the dying sun. Mutty, half strangled, kept on yelping.

"Let him go!" screamed Harrie. "Let him go!"

The gamekeeper looked down at her, eyes half shut, wearing a lazy smile. He had black hair that lay in strands across his forehead as if it were wet. "Yours, is he?" he asked.

"Yes. Please let him go. He wouldn't hurt anything, honestly he wouldn't."

"Ah, they all say that." He had a curious, singsong accent unfamiliar to Harrie. Suddenly he flung the dog towards her and in the same movement closed the gun and brought it up to his shoulder. "I'm within my rights to shoot," he said.

"You're not." Ian's voice came from just behind Harrie, to her immense relief. He sounded breathless, and she knew he was scared, but he went on bravely. "The dog's done no harm. And my dad says you should never point a gun at anyone."

"You know what your dad can do, don't you?" said the man deliberately.

"I wish old Cecil were still here," said Ian angrily.

"He was a *friend*," chimed in Harrie.

Neil clutched at her arm. "Come *on*," he said.

"Don't argue." He was staring at the gun, white-faced, and Harrie realized that he was terrified.

"It's all right, Neil," she said. "He won't shoot you. People don't."

But Neil turned and ran back along the path the way they had come, tearing along blindly until he caught his foot in a tree root and fell flat on his face.

"Idiot!" muttered Ian, going to see if Neil was all right. Harrie followed, holding Mutty by his collar. The gamekeeper stayed where he was, blocking the path into the wood, though he returned the gun to its position over his arm.

"I shan't warn you again!" he shouted after them. "Next time I'll mean business!"

Apart from a scratch on his face, Neil was not hurt. He patted about in the leaves for his glasses, which had fallen off, found them, put them on and got to his feet. He glanced nervously along the path, but the gamekeeper had disappeared.

"Sorry," he said. "I hate guns. Not used to them, I suppose."

Ian said nothing but led the way back along the path as if returning to the place where they had entered the wood. Then he turned sharply right, pushing his way through the tall bracken and ducking under silver birch branches.

"Ian," said Harrie. "Where are you going?"

"Home," said Ian.

"But—"

"I'm *not* going around by the quarry," said Ian obstinately. "We've always come through here and we've every right to. And anyway, the pheasants aren't breeding this time of the year—the young ones are nearly all full-grown. I don't know what he's fussing about."

Harrie, with Neil following, kept close behind her brother and held Mutty's collar tightly. The narrow, grassy path was hardly more than a rabbit's width, but soon it began to broaden out a little. The trees were thinner here, and in a few more yards the path opened into a clearing. Ian, still ahead of the others, took a couple of steps into the open space, then suddenly stopped. "Good Lord," he said.

"What is it?" Harrie caught up with him and gasped. "Oh, *Ian!*"

A man lay face down on the short, rabbit-nibbled grass, hands outflung. He wore a dirty green waterproof jacket and Wellington boots, and his head, which was toward the children, was completely bald except for a little fringe of gingery hair around the edge. A navy blue cotton cap lay on the grass beside him, and the bald head seemed to Harrie somehow horribly naked without it. In the fading, rosy daylight, it was as round and white as the dollop of ice cream on top of a cone.

Harrie found her voice. "Are you all right?" she asked the man. He made no answer, and Ian, frowning, walked around him cautiously. Then he moved nearer, squatted down and pushed carefully at the man's shoulder to try and turn him on his side.

A sudden, sickening burst of flies buzzed out and Ian jumped back. "He's dead," he said.

Neil waited for no more, but headed for the widest path out of the clearing, in full flight for the second time. Harrie followed, letting go of Mutty's collar in her panic. The dog paused only for a momentary sniff at the man before loping after them.

"This way!" gasped Ian. In a few minutes of frantic running they were out of the wood and tearing along the rutted lane that led to the farm, not stopping until they clattered into the yard. The warm, wet smell of the milking parlor was reassuring, and Ian slowed down to a walk as they crossed between the buildings. Harrie was too out of breath to say anything, but she took Ian's hand. Instead of laughing, he squeezed it. "It's all right," he said. "We'll tell the police."

"But who was it?" panted Neil.

Ian shrugged "No idea."

"Let's go home," begged Harrie.

Chapter 2
Where Is the Bald Man?

The policeman stirred his tea comfortably. "And you think this chap was dead?" he said.

"He *was* dead," corrected Ian.

Mrs. Armstrong gave her son a worried look. "Are you sure, Ian? He might have been a tramp, fast asleep, or he could have been drinking and passed out, perhaps. There are some funny people about. Will you have another scone?" she added to the policeman.

"No, thanks," he said. Dusting crumbs from his uniform, he added. "Who's going to show me this corpse, then?"

Harrie felt her face redden with anger because he so obviously didn't believe it, but she didn't want to go back to the wood, especially now that it was almost dark. Ian was putting on his parka. "I am," he said. "Coming, Neil?" Harrie was glad he didn't ask her. Ian could be very understanding sometimes.

"No, Neil can't go," said Mrs. Armstrong firmly. "I told his mum on the phone he'd be home in half an hour. She'll be worried enough as it is, with all this talk about corpses."

"*He was there*," said Harrie earnestly.

Everyone looked at her. The policeman said patiently, "When your mum rang up, I was informed by radio and asked to check. I was over at Thetbrook, but as soon as I'd finished there I came to your wood and had a good look around."

"I know," said Harrie. "You said."

"There was nobody about," the policeman continued, "dead *or* alive. I saw a white van going across the airfield in the distance, but that was all."

"I don't care," said Harrie obstinately. "He was *there*. We all saw him."

Mrs. Armstrong said kindly, "Of course he was there if you saw him, lovey. But he may not have been dead."

The back door opened. "Who was dead?" asked Mr. Armstrong, kicking off his Wellingtons. Everyone explained at once, and he listened without comment as he unzipped his overalls and peeled them off. He washed his hands, then sat down at the table and passed his cup across to his wife for tea. He stirred and sipped, then buttered a scone and finally said, "Ian's seen enough dead things to know if a man's dead or not."

"*Quite*," said Ian gratefully.

"You'd better go off and have a look," Mr. Armstrong added to the policeman, "while I have my tea."

"By all means," said the policeman, getting to his feet. "You can't be too careful. Come on, sonny."

Ian made a face at Harrie because of being called "sonny" and led the way out.

Harrie was glad to sit quietly in the warm kitchen with Neil while her father had his tea and her mother poured out another cup to keep him company. The thought of what had happened out there in the wood seemed like a bad dream.

"What did he look like, this chap?" asked her father.

"He was bald," said Harrie. "And he had Wellingtons on, and a shooting jacket like yours."

"Did you see his face?"

Harrie shook her head. "Ian did. He turned him over and—all flies flew out."

"He'd been injured, then," said her father. "Flies collect where there's blood."

"Ian said he'd been shot," said Harrie. "We just ran and ran, but afterwards he said the grass was all bloody underneath him."

"He had a funny hat," put in Neil. "It was on the grass beside him. Blue. Sort of like a yachting cap."

Mr. Armstrong shook his head, puzzled. "Nobody around here wears that sort of hat. Wonder who he was."

"You must all keep well away from there," said Mrs. Armstrong briskly as she started to clear the table. "Leave it to the police. Like I said, there's a lot of funny people around here these days. Look at these rustlers we keep hearing about. A farmer in Milton Parva lost a whole flock of sheep last week—and that's not far from here."

"Filthy business," agreed her husband. "They killed them in the field, you know, and took the carcasses. Left the skins and guts for the farmer to find in the morning. Did you know Agnew lost a bunch of steers?"

"No!" His wife was horrified. "That's only down the road! When did it happen?"

"On Monday night," said Mr. Armstrong. "Andrew only heard about it this morning when he happened to meet Mrs. Agnew in the bank. She said the funny thing about it is, they were away from home on Monday. They went to the dairy show and stayed overnight with her brother. Whoever did it must have known."

"The Milton Parva man was away, too," said

Mrs. Armstrong. "It said in the paper he had to go to a funeral."

"Looks as if it's somebody local," agreed Mr. Armstrong gloomily. "Or at least they're getting a local tip-off."

"That's awful!" said Harrie. "It might be someone we *know*!"

"It makes you feel you can't trust anybody," agreed her mother. "What are the police doing?"

Mr. Armstrong shrugged. "What *can* they do? They can't be everywhere at once. Andrew's calling a meeting tomorrow night to see if we can get up a patrol. He's been telephoning the local farms all day. I think everyone's coming."

Mrs. Armstrong nodded thoughtfully. "That's the ony way—to tackle it ourselves. If we all take a turn at patroling, one of us is bound to be in the right place sooner or later. I don't know what I'd do if it happened to be me that found them, though!"

"Oh, nobody goes out alone," said her husband. "Andrew thinks we should send two vehicles with four or five people in each. With shotguns."

Neil was looking puzzled. "Who's Andrew?" he asked.

"He's the farm manager where Dad works," explained Harrie. "Lea Farm—you know, where we came through the yard."

"I thought you said it belonged to Mr. Ashworth," said Neil.

"It does," said Harrie patiently. "But he's just a businessman. He doesn't even live at the farm."

Neil was even more confused. "Who does, then?"

Harrie sighed. "I'm telling you. Andrew Corrie, the farm manager. He does all the running of the farm. Mr. Ashworth only comes up here for the shooting, really."

"He stays at the old manor house on the far side of the farm when he's here," Mr. Armstrong explained. "His wife lives there part of the time, but she's more often at the London flat. And the girls are away at school, but they come here for the holidays—except when they're abroad."

Neil pushed his glasses up his snub nose and said, "What a funny way to live."

"Time you were off home, Neil," said Mrs. Armstrong.

Her husband got to his feet. "Where do you live, Neil?" he asked. "I'll run you home."

"Oh, no, it's all right," said Neil. "It's only five minutes' walk, around in Mill Gardens."

"I'll give you a lift," repeated Mr. Armstrong firmly. "Best to be on the safe side, and the Land Rover's still warm."

"Oh. Well, thanks very much," said Neil. Then

he added, "By the way, Ian said you were a member of the airplane-modelers club. I was wondering—"

They went out.

"Beastly model airplanes," said Harrie.

Mrs. Armstrong smiled at her daughter. "Keeps them out of mischief," she said.

Harrie nodded. The afternoon's events kept going through her mind. "That gamekeeper was really horrible, Mum," she said. "He threatened to shoot Mutty."

"Well, he's got his job to do," said her mother. "And with all these rustlers about, I suppose he feels he's got to be extra careful. Still, he does seem a funny sort of man. I don't see why Mr. Ashworth couldn't have found somebody local."

"Where does he come from, then?" asked Harrie.

"He's Welsh," said her mother. "His name's Mr. Selwyn. Didn't you notice the accent?"

"Oh," said Harrie. "Is that what it was."

Headlights streamed across the window and car doors slammed. Ian came into the kitchen followed by the policeman, who said smugly, "The corpse got up and walked away, it seems."

"No!" Harrie couldn't believe it. "Ian, he *must* be there! Are you sure you found the right place?"

"Of course I'm sure," said Ian angrily. "I know

every inch of that wood. We went straight to the clearing and all that was left was the remains of a trash fire, what looked like a whole lot of old wood and sacks and things, right on the spot where the man had been."

Harrie gasped. "You don't mean—"

"There was nobody *in* the bonfire, miss," interrupted the policeman. "That was perfectly plain to see." He unbuttoned his pocket and took out a notebook. "Now, there's no need to take a statement at present, but if I could just have a note of the names . . . Ian—?"

"Armstrong," supplied Ian.

"And the other boy?"

"Neil Grey."

"Address?"

"It's the last house in Mill Gardens. I don't know the number."

"Mill Gardens. That's the new development, isn't it?"

"Yes."

"And this is—Lea Farm Cottage. Your name, miss?"

"Harriet Armstrong."

"Good." The policeman finished writing and put away his notebook. "I don't suppose I shall have to bother you again. Thank you for the tea, Mrs. Armstrong."

"You're welcome," she said politely.

The Land Rover came into the yard behind the house as the policeman was leaving. Mr. Armstrong got out and said, "Well?"

"No sign of a corpse, sir, you'll be glad to hear."

"Only a dirty great bonfire," put in Ian.

Mr. Armstrong looked from the policeman to Ian, then back again. "I don't know that I am glad to hear it," he said. "It seems to me there's something funny going on, and I hope you're taking it seriously."

"We take everything seriously, sir," said the policeman. "I have notified headquarters of this incident by radio and a thorough check will be made. We have a good description of the man and we'll watch out for him."

"But he's *dead*," said Ian.

The policeman gave him a disparaging look and added to Mr. Armstrong, "I'll be on my way, then, sir. Good night."

"Good night," they all said.

Back in the kitchen, Mr. Armstrong sat down heavily and stared at Ian, frowning.

"What the heck's going on?" he said, more to himself than to anyone else.

Ian said, "Dad, he *was* dead. It's like that cow that died of bloat last year—they look quite different when they're not alive anymore. I *know* he was dead."

"It's all right," said his father. "I believe you. I told young Neil he could come up to the airfield with us tomorrow to fly the planes, and we'll have a good look around."

"I'll come too," said Harrie bravely. "And Mutty."

"You'd better bring his lead," said her father.

Harrie laughed. "He'll be terribly offended. He hasn't been on a lead since he was a puppy."

But lead or no lead, she thought, it would be nice to have Mutty there. Just in case.

Chapter 3
Tire Tracks

They had just finished lunch on Saturday when Neil arrived with his mother. Except that she wore her hair in an untidy bun, she looked exactly like Neil, with a round face and spectacles and a rather popeyed look. She had the same sort of squeaky voice, too.

"I couldn't *believe* it!" she said. "In a quiet little village like this, to find a murdered man in a wood—it's worse than London!"

"Who says he was murdered?" asked Mr. Armstrong.

"He must have been," said Mrs. Grey. "It's awful. We never had corpses in Clapham. What did the police say when they saw him?"

"They didn't," said Harrie. "He'd gone."

"Gone? You mean he wasn't dead after all?" Mrs. Grey sounded rather disappointed.

"We don't really know," said Mr. Armstrong. "We'll have to look around this afternoon. Is all the stuff in the Land Rover, Ian?"

"Yes," said Ian. "It's been ready for hours." He had his parka on and was obviously waiting to go.

Mr. Armstrong got to his feet. "Right," he said. "Come on, Neil. You coming with us, Harrie?"

"Yes," said Harrie. Mutty's lead was already stuffed into her pocket.

"Neil, you will be careful, won't you?" said his mother anxiously. "Don't go doing anything silly."

"I'm sure they won't," said Mrs. Armstrong soothingly. "What about a cup of tea? There's one in the pot."

"Oh, well, just a quickie," said Mrs. Grey, perching uneasily on the edge of the bench seat by the table.

"See you later," said Ian firmly and led the way out to the Land Rover.

"Ernie's flying his helicopter," said Ian, squinting up into the sky as they got out onto the cracked tarmac.

"Coo!" said Neil. "I've never seen a model helicopter. Are they difficult?"

"Terrible things," said Mr. Armstrong. "Slip about all over the place. I'd rather have a little stunt plane any time."

"Shall we go and look?" asked Harrie, "Or are you going to fly first?"

Her father smiled at her worried face. "Come on," he said. "Let's get it over." Somebody waved and shouted, "You flying today?" and Mr. Armstrong shouted back, "In a minute. Just take the dog for a walk."

Harrie clipped Mutty's lead to his collar, and he hurled himself forward against the unaccustomed restraint, uttering loud, choking noises. "He is awful on the lead," said Harrie.

"Tap him on the nose," advised her father. "Here." He took Mutty's lead in a firm grip and shouted, "Heel!" but Mutty, to Harrie's secret amusement, took no notice and they progressed toward the wood at an undignified gallop.

Ian led them unhesitatingly to the clearing. A burned patch extended almost all the way across it, ashy and unpromising. Mr. Armstrong bent down and felt the ground cautiously. "Still hot," he said. "Must have been quite a fire."

Ian was stirring the ashes with the toe of his boot. "Not a sign," he said bitterly. "You'd never know there'd been blood on the grass. Not now that it's all burned."

Mr. Armstrong looked at his son. "You're sure this is the clearing?" he asked. "Another one would look much the same."

Ian clenched his fists. "Of *course* I'm sure!" he shouted. "I thought at least *you* believed me!"

Mr. Armstrong shook his head, perplexed. "I don't know what to think," he said. "I do believe you—of course I do. But there's nothing here, is there?"

"No," admitted Ian. "Not now."

"And we can't search the whole wood," his father went on reasonably. "It would take us days."

"And we'd never get to fly the plane," put in Neil.

Mr. Armstrong smiled at him. "All right," he said. "I'm just coming. Let's leave the mystery for today, Ian. This isn't the end of it, I'm sure. Something else'll turn up. It always does, just when you're least expecting it."

Ian stared at the ashes gloomily, unconvinced.

"Come on," said his father. "Let's go and fly the plane."

Neil ran after him, but Ian stayed where he was, hands in pockets and shoulders hunched despondently. Harrie gazed at him. "I wish there was something I could do," she said.

"There isn't," said Ian and trailed away after the others, kicking at clumps of grass. Harrie followed.

At the edge of the wood Ian stopped suddenly. He bent down and stared at the ground, and said, "Harrie, look!"

"What is it?" she asked.

"Tire tracks. See where they stop? Someone has driven as close to the wood as they could get. A van's been backed up to the end of the path . . . then driven away again."

"You mean—to collect something."

"Or someone." Ian and Harrie stared at each other, each imagining the grim, furtive loading of a corpse into the back of a van . . . or a car, or a truck.

"How wide was it?" Ian began to pace the distance between the two tracks, putting one foot carefully in front of the other so that his heel touched his toe each time.

"And what may you be doing?" asked a sarcastic voice from above them. Harrie gasped. The gamekeeper stood only a few paces away, his gun held in both hands, ready to fire.

"Just looking at something," said Ian, standing up.

"And just what were you looking at?"

"Tire tracks," said Harrie and immediately regretted it. Mr. Selwyn, she remembered, didn't know they had seen the dead man, so there was no reason to be interested in a vehicle that might have moved him. And she mustn't make him suspicious.

"We're . . . we're interested in tread patterns,"

she invented wildly. "All the different sorts. Dad's got great, big, thick ones on his Land Rover."

"It's a project for school," said Ian, coming to Harrie's rescue. "A sort of survey. To see what kinds of tires are most popular. Cross-ply and radials and all that. Er . . . what sort of vehicle made these tracks, do you know?"

Mr. Selwyn eyed them narrowly for a few moments, then said, "My Mini van. Unloading barley for the birds, if it's anything to do with you. Where's that dog of yours?"

"He's with Dad," said Harrie, looking around to confirm this statement. To her relief, she saw that her father and Neil were coming back. Mutty was still tugging at his lead.

"What's up?" asked Mr. Armstrong as he approached.

"Are these your children?" demanded the gamekeeper.

"They are. Not causing any trouble, I hope?"

"Not today, no. But I had to warn them yesterday that I won't have that dog running loose in here."

"So I heard," said Mr. Armstrong. He looked at the gamekeeper thoughtfully and added, "Get many poachers around here, do you?"

"Not many," said Mr. Selwyn carefully.

"None in the last few days . . . yesterday, for instance?"

"No. What's it to do with you, anyway?"

"Nothing at all," said Mr. Armstrong easily. "Just that we've had the police at the farm, asking if we've seen any strangers about. I'm glad they're taking an interest. With this blasted rustling going on, you can't be too careful."

"No," agreed the gamekeeper. "We all of us got to be careful, haven't we?" His eyes were flitting along the treetops as he spoke, and with a suddenness that shocked Harrie he brought the gun to his shoulder and fired. The deafening crash echoed through the wood, sending birds screeching up from the trees, but Harrie still heard the soft rustle and thud of a small body falling to the ground. "Squirrel," said the gamekeeper. "Not many of them around here, but that's one less. I'll go and get it."

"What for?" asked Ian.

The man gave him a tight-lipped smile. "Nail it to my gibbet," he said. "As a warning to the others." And with a small gesture of touching a nonexistent cap, he turned and was gone.

Neil had clapped his hands to his ears when the shot was fired and only now cautiously took them down. His face was white. "I don't think I like this airfield," he said. "I wish I'd stuck to going around by the road."

Mr. Armstrong laughed. "Poor old Neil," he said. "Come on. Let's fly the airplane. Nothing frightening about that."

"Hang on a minute, Dad," said Ian. "You see these tire tracks—are they made by a Mini?"

"No," scoffed his father. "Much too wide apart. More like a Bedford or a Transit. Come on or we'll lose the best of the light."

Following their father, Ian and Harrie exchanged significant glances. Why had the gamekeeper lied?

Chapter 4
A Meeting

The model airplanes darted about in the sky, their little engines buzzing angrily. Their earthbound owners gazed up as they clutched the magic boxes that transmitted their instructions, every touch of the control lever producing an obedient movement in the flying model. A tuft of colored ribbon waved from each aerial to indicate which radio frequency was being used.

Mutty whined and scratched irritably at his collar as if trying to free himself from the irksome lead. "All right," Harrie said to him. "We'll go for a walk."

Neil and Ian were crouched over a grounded model, exploring its innards with a screwdriver. "I'm going to take Mutty for a walk," Harrie told them. "Not in the wood. Just across the airfield. Do you want to come?"

Ian shook his head, absorbed in what he was doing, and Neil said, beaming, "I'm going to have a go at flying the plane in a minute!"

"Oh," said Harrie. "All right. I won't be long."

Neither of the boys replied, so she set off across the runway with Mutty. When they were well clear of the model airplanes, she let the dog off the lead. He shook himself thoroughly, from his head down to his tail, and set off at an exploring trot. Harrie followed him. Walks were much more fun when Mutty chose where to go. A rabbit bolted out from a bramble thicket and Mutty shot after it, waving his tail ecstatically. The rabbit bounced along, leaping from side to side, and reached a derelict building only just ahead of the dog. They both disappeared from sight around the corner. Harrie followed. The building was a big one, still retaining part of its roof. There were glassless windows at intervals along its length, and at the far end the remains of double doors leaned open. Oddly, half the width of the entrance was blocked off with a wall of straw bales.

"Mutty!" called Harrie. The dog appeared at once around the end of the wall of bales and wagged his tail—then went back into the building. "Oh, Mutty!" said Harrie, exasperated. "What have you got in there?" It was rather dark inside, because straw bales had been stacked across each window as if to exclude the rain, or, Harrie thought, to protect the contents from inquiring glances. For standing in the shadowed quiet of the building was a large, wooden-sided cattle truck.

Harrie felt the back of her neck prickle. Rustlers. This would be the ideal spot to hide a cattle truck. She walked around it cautiously, peering in through the slatted sides. It was empty, but it had not been hosed down since it last held animals. Dirty straw stuck out all the way along at floor level. Harrie walked around to the cab and looked on the door to see who it belonged to. Trucking firms usually had their names lettered boldly on a headboard over the cab or along the doors, but this vehicle bore no trace of an owner's name. Above the cab window were two paintings of horses' heads facing inward toward the black letters that simply said, "Horses." Harrie frowned. She knew that the operator's name and address had to be shown on the outside of the truck. But this one was blank. Perhaps it was an old one, no longer in use. She stood on tiptoe and stared up at the license plate on the windshield. No, it was for the current year.

Mutty wandered up, wearing the offhand look of a dog that has lost a rabbit—and at that moment Harrie heard a car coming. It was probably one of the model-airplane people, she told herself, in search of a crashed plane. The beastly little things always seemed to go out of control sooner or later. But the car sounded as if it were coming from the other way; from the quarry side of the airfield. It came close to the building and stopped outside. The engine was switched off, and doors slammed. Someone was coming in.

Desperately Harrie dragged at the straw bales, trying to pull them away from the window to make a gap behind them where she could hide. They were damp and heavy, and the top bales wobbled perilously, threatening to fall off. Harrie could hear the unknown people coming to the building's entrance. The gap behind the bales was barely big enough to admit her, but Harrie crammed herself into the damp, earwiggy crevice, dragging Mutty after her. Jammed upright in the narrow crack, she whispered, "Ssh!" and felt her way down the dog's head until her fingers closed around his muzzle. As if sensing her anxiety, he wriggled as close to Harrie as he could and kept perfectly still.

"I don't like it," a man's voice was saying. "Not one bit, see. I don't know if those kids saw anything, but there'll be trouble if they did." The Welsh accent was unmistakable. It was the gamekeeper.

Another voice said wearily, "My dear chap, you

can't possibly imagine that I'll change my plans for a couple of snotty nosed kids?"

"We can't do it without Baldy," objected Selwyn. "And talking of that, what have you done about him, anyway?"

"Baldy?" The other man laughed. "Shall we say—Baldy is keeping cool. As we all should, Taffy." Then he stopped laughing. "Nobody is indispensable, Selwyn," he said, with an icy edge to his voice. "Remember that. And don't imagine that you can stop playing the game, old chap. Once in, you stay in. That was Baldy's mistake,

wasn't it? And you saw what happened to him—
didn't you?"

Harrie heard Selwyn clear his throat nervously.
"Oh, yes," he said. "Yes, I did. I wasn't meaning
. . . to get out, or anything. I just thought perhaps
we'd put it off for a bit. Till we get another driver,
like."

"I've *got* another driver," said the first man,
sounding bored with such a simple matter. "Very
reliable chap. A Belgian. You can call him Brown."

"Baldy was a Belgian, wasn't he?" said Selwyn.

"Just forget about Baldy," said the man coldly.
"Try and keep your stupid mind on the business. I
will arrive in the van, bringing the driver. You
bring the truck around to the field—no headlights,
remember—then we load up and Brown drives it
to the port. I follow in the van. I've got chaps waiting there to take over. They'll see it all through to
the other side as usual. You shut the gate, leave
everything tidy, and get off to the pub. Play darts,
get drunk, get yourself noticed."

"Create an alibi," said Selwyn gloomily.

"Quite. Any questions?"

"No," said Selwyn. "I just hope to God it
works."

"It always works," said the other man impa-
tiently. "By the time they're on the high seas I'll be
drinking whisky with old Ashworth in his club.

When he finds out, the last person he'll suspect is his old school chum. You don't understand the old boy network, Selwyn."

"Don't want to," muttered Selwyn. "Long as I get paid, that's all."

"You'll get paid," said the other man with contempt. "You've never *not* been paid, have you? Now, nip off and fiddle with your pheasants, or whatever it is you do. Look normal."

Harrie so much wanted to see what the other man looked like that she almost forgot her fear. Very cautiously, she pushed at the bales in front of her to try and make a crack between them so that she could see out. Mutty, who had been sitting in a cramped position, took Harrie's movement to be a sign that they were going out and turned himself around energetically, rustling the straw. Harrie heard the click of the shotgun closing as the gamekeeper snapped, "Who's there?"

"Oh, put it down, Selwyn," said the other man tiredly. "You rustics are all so damned trigger-happy. It's only a rat. You should be like me— stick to human rats. Much more sporting. Now, come along."

Harrie heard them leave the building. She dared not move again until the engine of the vehicle outside started up, then she stood on tiptoe and looked out of the window. The vehicle was not a car. It was an ice cream van with a sliding window in its side—but the pictures of ice cream that decorated it had been obliterated with white paint, crudely splashed on so that the cones and popsicles were still visible as faint ghosts under their white veil.

Harrie's first instinct was to follow the van and see where it went, but she realized that the minute she went around the edge of the building to see the van, the men in it would be able to see her. She decided to stay where she was.

When the sound of the engine had faded away completely, Harrie ventured out. Mutty bounded ahead of her, making a nonsense of her fears. The airfield was as empty and deserted as ever, the little group of model-airplane enthusiasts and their cars dwarfed by the wide sky. The conversation in the building seemed too fantastic to be true. Had she imagined it? Harrie glanced back at the building, its broken windows with the bales behind them staring like sightless eyes. No, she had not imagined it.

She must tell Ian quickly, Harrie thought. He would know what to do. She set off across the tarmac at a run.

Chapter 5
The Plan

The boys were packing batteries and bits of wire and bottles of fuel into a large wooden box.

"Hello," said Ian, looking up as Harrie arrived, panting. "You've been a long time. Had a good walk?" Harrie was too out of breath to reply and Ian went on, "Dad's having a go with Ernie's helicopter. He says he doesn't like them, but I think he does, really."

"Ian," gasped Harrie, "there's a cattle truck—in a building. And I heard—the gamekeeper—talking to a man. They're the rustlers!"

"No!" Ian was impressed. "How do you know?"

Harrie repeated the conversation she had heard in the building. Ian listened carefully and Neil, squatting on his heels by the box, stared up at Harrie round-eyed and open-mouthed. "How *awful!*" he said, when Harrie had told them everything she could remember. "What shall we do? Tell the police?"

Ian frowned. "I don't think there's much point," he said. "To start with, Harrie was on her own when she heard all this—"

"Mutty was there," interrupted Harrie.

"Yes, but Mutty can't talk," Ian explained patiently. "And the police may think Harrie is making it up. You can see they didn't believe us about the bald man. And even if they do believe her, there's not much to go on. What did he actually *say*, Harrie, this snooty-sounding bloke? Did he mention a particular time or a day? And are you absolutely sure he was talking about *our* cattle and *this* airfield?"

"No," admitted Harrie. "But he must have meant somewhere near here because he said, 'bring the cattle truck around to the field,' as if it wasn't far to go. And he told the gamekeeper to go to the pub so as to have an alibi. And he mentioned 'old Ashworth' and said he went to school with him."

Ian shook his head. "It's not enough," he said. "They'll write it all down and go away and do nothing about it. You know what they'll say. 'An imaginative little girl—you can see she thinks it's all real.' And you can't prove it, Harrie."

Harrie had a sour taste in her mouth from being

so out of breath, and her chest hurt. "But, Ian," she said, almost in tears, "we must do something. I didn't imagine it, honestly I didn't."

"Of course you didn't," said Ian at once. "I know that. We just need a bit more, that's all. Just some real piece of evidence."

"But what?" asked Neil, looking rather scared.

"I don't know," said Ian. "Perhaps we can come back here after tea, when everyone's gone home. We'll ask Dad."

"Doesn't he have to milk the cows?" asked Neil.

"Not on the weekend," said Harrie. "There's a relief milker comes in. It'll be dark by about seven, though, Ian. We won't be able to see anything."

"Yes, we will," said Ian. "We'll have finished tea soon after six, so we can call for Neil and come straight on up here. It isn't as dark as it looks when you're in the house with the light on. I was littering calf pens with Dad last week, and we could still see what we were doing at nearly eight o'clock."

"I think you're awfully brave," said Neil. "I don't think I want to come up here in the dark."

"Being frightened is exciting," said Ian. "Go on, Neil, don't chicken out. We'll pick you up at about half past six. If Dad says it's OK, that is. We'll have to ask him."

"Ask him what?" inquired Mr. Armstrong,

coming up with Ernie Hayden and the model helicopter, which looked much bigger in his hands
than it did in the sky. "Here, you should try one
of these, Ian. They really are a test of skill. I think I
might build one."

"Dad," said Harrie, "there's a cattle truck hidden in one of the buildings."

"That'll be Mr. Ashworth's horse van," said Mr.
Armstrong. "His daughters use it for their
ponies—go all over the place on weekends. Gym-
khanas and I don't know what."

"But it's got no license plate or any name on it,"
said Harrie. "And it hasn't been washed down
since it was used last. And it doesn't smell like
horses."

"I don't think anyone would bother Mr. Ashworth," said her father. "Everybody knows him.
And you know what those girls are like—think
more of plaiting their ponies' manes and buying
fancy tack than they do of hosing down the horse
van."

"I thought commercial vehicles were supposed
to have a name on, though," objected Ian.

"Last I heard, the old man was going to have the
whole thing repainted and done up with gold lines
and all that," said Mr. Armstrong. "I suppose he'll
get the name put on then."

"Oh," said Harrie, dashed. She tried again. "But

the gamekeeper came in, Dad, with another man. And they were talking about Baldy being dead—that must be the man we saw, mustn't it? And they've got a plan to steal some cattle."

Ernie Hayden grinned broadly. "All this talk of rustling must have gone to her head, I reckon," he said. "You want to watch it, Bill, or she'll have you dashing around the airfield all night looking for villains."

"Not tonight, she won't," said Mr. Armstrong as he handed the helicopter back to Ernie. "We're going to a meeting at the farm to organize a patrol system. These rustlers aren't kids' stuff." He looked at Harrie's agitated face and put his hand on her shoulder. "Don't look so worried," he added. "You may be onto something really important, and if it is, we'll go straight to the police. You can tell me all about it on the way home."

"Shall we start packing the stuff in the Land Rover, Dad?" asked Ian.

"Yes, please," said his father. "I just want to have a word with Ernie about this helicopter, then I'll be over."

Ian and Neil picked up the box and Harrie went with them to the Land Rover, accompanied as always by Mutty.

"What shall we do?" she asked.

Ian stared around the airfield with narrowed

eyes. Then he said, "We'll go just the same."

They loaded the box into the back of the Land Rover, and Ian slammed the tail gate shut. "I don't suppose we'll find anything," he said. "But you never know. It just needs one definite thing, and the police would really sit up and take notice. Half past six, Neil?"

Neil turned pink. "I know you'll think I'm a coward," he said, "and I am. But, honestly, the thought of being up here in the dark makes me feel all wobbly." Then an idea struck him. "Tell you what, though—I can see right over the airfield from my bedroom window. After tea I'll go up there with the light out and watch. If you take a flashlight with you, you can flash it if anything goes wrong, and I'll see it."

"Yes, we will!" said Harrie gratefully. "We can take Dad's big flashlight that he does the evening rounds with—you can see that a mile off."

"Three flashes means we're in trouble," said Ian.

"What should I do?" asked Neil.

Ian grinned. "I don't know," he said. "Whatever you can think of. Tell your dad. Call the cops. Scream for help. Drop dead with fright."

"*Ian!*" said Harrie.

"Well, he's such a twit," said Ian. "Come on, there's Dad waving. We'd better get the rest of this stuff packed or we'll be home late for tea and it'll all go wrong."

"We're having crumpets," said Neil.

"No wonder you're fat," said Ian.

Harrie sometimes despaired of her brother.

Mrs. Armstrong cut slices of sticky, black gingerbread still warm from the oven and said, "Well, I don't know, Harrie. It certainly sounds as if *something* is going on."

"Trouble is," said Harrie's father thoughtfully, "it's so easy to put two and two together and make about six and a half. Things don't usually fit as neatly as they seem to. All the same, what you heard sounds pretty odd. I'll tell them about it at the meeting tonight and I'll go around to the police station in the morning—or we might drop in now, come to think of it. There's just about time." He turned to his wife. "Jean, are you coming to this meeting?"

"You bet I am," said Mrs. Armstrong. "I can drive a Land Rover, same as anyone else."

"Right," said her husband. "The more the merrier. But we'd better get a move on." He drank his tea, then said seriously, "Now, listen, you two. This rustling business isn't a game. Whoever is doing it, they're not fools and they're certainly dangerous. So don't go looking for trouble—

especially you, Ian. Stay here and watch the television, so we'll know you're safe."

"But, Dad," said Harrie, "we nearly always take Mutty for a walk after tea."

"Just a short walk," chimed in Ian. "And we might as well just have a *look* on the airfield. If we see anyone about, we'll come straight back and ring you up."

"Well ..." Mr. Armstrong hesitated. "I don't suppose you can come to any harm at this time of day. But keep out of the wood."

"And don't stay out after dark," said Mrs. Armstrong.

"We won't," promised Harrie.

Mr. Armstrong glanced at the clock on the wall. "Ten to six," he said. "Come on, Jean—you'd better hurry if you want to change or anything."

Mrs. Armstrong looked down at her corduroy trousers and said, "I think I'll go as I am. It's not really a social occasion, is it? Harrie and Ian," she added, "will you do the washing up for me? We'll be late otherwise, especially if we're going to the police station first."

"Of course we will," said Harrie.

Her parents put their coats on, and Mr. Armstrong turned at the door. "Now, don't forget," he said. "Straight back here after your walk."

"Straight back," promised Ian.

When the Land Rover had gone, Harrie said, "Shall we wash up now, or when we come back?"

"Now," said Ian. "And not too quickly. The later we go the more chance there is of seeing something."

"Oh, Ian!" Harrie scolded him. "We *must* go soon. We promised we'd be in before dark."

"So we will be," said Ian. He tipped the water out of the saucepan that stood soaking in the sink and shook his head sorrowfully. "Scrambled egg does stick so. Takes *ages* to get clean."

Harrie tried to look disapproving, but she felt so excited—and a little scared—that she couldn't help giggling. She cleared the dishes from the table and picked up a dish towel to help Ian with the drying.

At last everything was clean. The cups were on their hooks, the saucers and plates in their places in the cupboard, knives and forks away in their drawer, and the tablecloth shaken free of crumbs and folded up. Ian took the big flashlight from the shelf by the back door and switched it on to be sure that it was working. Its beam flashed a dazzling light across the ceiling, and Mutty got up from his place by the stove, yawned, stretched, and sat expectantly by the door.

"*You're* not coming," said Ian.

"Oh, yes, he is," said Harrie firmly. "I'm not

going without him." She now felt very much more scared than excited and was beginning to wish she had never said anything about the cattle truck and the rustlers.

Ian looked at her and said, "Oh, all right, then. But keep him on the lead. Better put your parka on. It may be cold up there."

"I know," said Harrie. Ian could be bossy sometimes, but tonight it was quite nice to be bossed. It made her feel less frightened.

"Ready?" asked Ian. Harrie nodded. They went out, closing the back door carefully behind them.

As Ian had said, it was hardly dark at all outside.

"It's just right," said Ian quietly. "We won't need the flashlight for ages yet."

"Perhaps not at all," said Harrie hopefully.

Ian ignored this remark. "If there's anybody up there," he went on, "they won't expect anyone to be looking for them as early as this."

"I hope they can't hear us," Harrie whispered back. In the fading daylight, everything seemed very quiet. The crunch of their footsteps down the gravel path, and even Mutty's panting breath as he pulled against his lead, sounded terribly loud. They went out of the garden gate, across the lane to the farm, through the deserted yard, and started along the track that led up to the airfield.

Chapter 6
The Cattle Truck

It seemed darker as they climbed up the sloping path, probably because the hedges were so high, shutting out the sky. In the places where trees grew in dense clumps it would be difficult, Harrie thought uneasily, to see if anyone was there. Something rustled suddenly in the dead leaves beside the path, and Mutty rushed across to investigate, dragging Harrie with him by his lead. It turned out to be a sleepy hedgehog, and Mutty danced around it, barking furiously.

"Shut *up!*" said Ian, hauling the dog away. "I knew we should have left him at home, Harrie—he's going to be an awful nuisance."

"He hates hedgehogs," said Harrie. "They prickle his nose. You know what a fuss he makes if he finds one in the garden."

Ian frowned at the dog. "I don't know. Perhaps we'd better take him back to the house."

"No," said Harrie.

Ian shrugged. "Oh, all right. What the heck—there won't be anyone there anyway."

"I hope there won't," said Harrie. "In a way. Though it would be nice to prove that we were right."

As they approached the wood, Ian said, "I suppose you want to go around by the quarry lane?"

"Yes, we must," said Harrie. "Dad said." To her relief, Ian made no objection. Skirting the dark wood, they set off along the path that ran around the outside of it and led into the lane.

"I wonder if Neil's watching?" said Harrie.

"Probably too scared even to watch," said Ian scornfully. "Honestly, what a twit."

"I think he's rather nice," said Harrie. "He's sort of funny—and he knows he is, and he doesn't mind. And fancy *saying* you're a coward! I wouldn't dare admit it."

"But, then, you're not a coward," said Ian.

Harrie thought privately that she was not so sure about that, but decided not to say so. They walked on until they came to the lane and turned left, toward the quarry and the airfield. Although the wide sky looked a paler blue here, all the solid things seemed to merge together in the dusk. They passed the place where a concrete slope led down into the quarry and went on up the lane. There was a steep drop on their right, marked off by a wooden fence that was half hidden by thickets of blackberry.

"I hope nobody *does* try messing about with our cattle," said Ian. "Apart from anything else, if they opened the gate and let them out, that old fence would never hold them. They'd just go crashing down into the quarry."

Harrie shuddered at the thought. "How *awful*," she said. She peered closely at the fence and pushed at it with her hand. "You're quite right," she added. "It *is* rickety. I mean, *I* couldn't break it, but the cattle could, easily. Mr. Ashworth ought to get it replaced."

"Don't expect he knows," said Ian. "He's not a proper farmer, is he? Spends half his time in London. I don't think he's interested in the place much, except for his pheasants. He likes to have his smart friends down for a weekend shoot, but that's about all. I wouldn't be like that if I was rich. I wouldn't have a farm manager—I'd want to see to things myself."

They came to the gateway into the cattle field on their left, just across the lane from the quarry's edge, and Ian said, "Hang on a minute." He went across to the gate and inspected it carefully, picking up the chain and padlock that secured it and tugging at them to make sure they were firm. "I'll just see if the cattle are all right," he said to Harrie. "Won't be long." He climbed over the gate and disappeared behind the hedge. Harrie stroked Mutty's head, glad of his comforting presence. It would have been awful here alone.

Directly opposite the gate there was a turnout where a tractor could be left without blocking the lane when Andrew brought feed blocks or barley straw up for the cattle. Harrie stared across at it, thinking of the summer two years ago when there was wheat growing in the field where the cattle were now. Her father had driven the combine harvester home when the field was finished and Harrie had ridden beside him on the narrow driving platform. It was like being on the deck of a ship, she remembered, standing so high up and looking out across the sea of stubble. And the combine was so wide that it took up both turnout and lane when it turned around. That was an awful moment, looking down straight into the depths of the quarry from such a height. She felt her stomach lurch again at the thought. But at least it had been warm then, with the late sun still hot on their backs—not like this chilly autumn evening.

Ian climbed back over the gate. "They're all right," he reported, jumping down onto the grass beside Harrie. "Now—where do we look first?"

"I don't know," said Harrie. "If the cattle truck *is* just Mr. Ashworth's horse van, there's no point in looking at that." She was beginning to feel depressed about the whole business.

Ian thought for a minute, then said, "We'll go and have a look, anyway. After all, that's where you heard the men talking. You never know, they might be there again. Which building was it?"

"You know where the straw stacks are?" said Harrie. "Down at the end of the runway? Well, it's past there, right on the edge of the airfield."

"I know where you mean," said Ian. "We can cut straight across. No need to go up to the model-airplane place."

They set off again. Harrie felt better now that she knew where they were going. The grass was long and dry here, almost knee-high, growing wild in the open wasteland of the airfield, some distance from the concrete runway. Although she walked carefully, Harrie occasionally caught her foot in one of the long bramble branches that snaked about on the ground and several times stumbled and nearly fell. The light was fading now and it was difficult to see any detail, but the building they were approaching stood out as a dark rectangle against the deep blue sky.

"Better be quiet now," muttered Ian. "If there's

anyone there, we don't want them to hear us."

"OK," breathed Harrie.

They emerged from the long grass onto the remains of a concrete pathway.

"Peri road," whispered Ian.

"What's that?"

"Road that went around the perimeter of the airfield. Now, pick your feet up, Harrie, and stop falling over things."

"But I can't help—" began Harrie in protest.

"Ssh!" hissed Ian.

They approached the building very quietly. When they reached it, they paused outside and listened. There was dead silence. "Nobody there," breathed Ian. Feeling his way, he moved inside the wall of straw bales, Harrie and Mutty close behind him. Inside, all daylight was blocked out by the straw bales across the windows, and it was very dark.

"I'm going to switch the flash on," whispered Ian.

The sudden light was dazzling. Harrie grabbed at Ian's arm. "It's gone!" she said. The straw bales were undisturbed and a few rat droppings littered the floor—but the building was otherwise empty. The cattle truck had gone.

Ian frowned. "That really *is* odd," he said. "Be-

cause Mr. Ashworth isn't here—he's been in London all this month. Mrs. Ashworth is with him and the girls are away at boarding school. So who moved the truck?"

Harrie stared at her brother, wide-eyed. "Ian," she said, "there really *is* something awful going on. We'd better go home and ring up Dad."

Ian nodded slowly as he looked around the empty building. "There must be," he agreed. "I mean, it was here this afternoon. They must have taken it for a job tonight. But where? Yes, we'd better tell Dad straight away. We can call in at the farm on our way back—it'll be quicker. We'll go the other way back across the airfield, though. If anyone's driving the cattle truck, they'll have to stick to the runway. We might see it."

"We can't use the flashlight to look for it," said Harrie, worried. "It's all right in here, because the light couldn't be seen from outside, but if Neil sees any flash of light he'll think we're in trouble. And we're not—are we?"

"Of course not," said Ian firmly. "We'll be able to see without the flash. There was a full moon last night, so it'll be nearly full again tonight—plenty of light to see a cattle truck by. Come on."

He switched the flashlight off, and the velvety darkness seemed to press against Harrie's eyes. Mutty made a confident rush toward the lighter square of the door, dragging Harrie with him. Ian was close at their heels.

It was much less dark outside, but night seemed to have crept closer during the time they were in the building, and the moon that Ian had promised had not yet appeared.

"It's much easier walking on the runway," said Harrie as they set out again. "I hate those black-berries. The prickles go right through my socks. My legs are all scratched." There didn't seem any need to whisper now.

"You should have worn Wellies," said Ian, who never wore anything else on his feet if he could help it. "You can barge through the blackberries then." He had his hands in his pockets, striding out with a new confidence, and Harrie suspected that he was just as relieved to be going home as she was.

"We must hurry," she said. "We promised we'd be home before dark."

"We will be," said Ian. "Well—before pitch dark, anyway."

A cold wind had begun to blow, and it seemed a long time before they reached the place where they had been flying model airplanes earlier that day. It was all very different now, in the dusk. No movement and no sound. Were the ghosts stirring in the empty buildings, Harrie wondered—and pulled her mind away from such imaginings. Live human beings could be much more dangerous than dead ones. Ian glanced around briefly and said, "Deserted."

"Yes," agreed Harrie. "And no sign of the cattle truck. Come on—let's get home."

They turned left, joining the usual route they took on their way home from school, approaching the edge of the airfield where the quarry lane led down to the wood and then to the farm. Now that their expedition was nearly over and the unknown danger had come to nothing, Harrie felt much happier. Although it was now almost completely dark, the air was warmer here in the lane where the hedges on either side screened them from the cold wind.

As they approached the field where Ian had climbed the gate, Harrie thought comfortably about the black-and-white cattle lying down for the night, warm and drowsy on the grass. It must be quite nice to be a bullock, she mused, chewing the cud for hour after sleepy hour, sheltered from the wind by the thick hedge.

"Not so far now," said Ian cheerfully. "Another ten minutes and we'll be—" Then he stopped dead. Harrie saw it at the same time. Backed into the gateway to the field where Ian's beloved bullocks were stood the dark, featureless slab of the cattle truck.

Chapter 7
Desperate Measures

Ian grabbed Harrie's hand and pulled her after him down the bank, away from the open lane where, even in the dark, they could so easily be seen. Harrie dragged Mutty down beside them, her arm around his furry neck. She prayed that he would not choose this moment to find a hedgehog.

Suddenly the moon beamed out from behind a low bank of cloud. Harrie gave a stifled gasp. "Look!" she breathed. "The ice cream van!" Clearly visible now, the white van was backing into the turnout. "Got no lights on," Ian whispered back. "No wonder we didn't see anything. Bet the cattle truck didn't have lights, either."

Harrie nodded at him, remembering only now that the man in the building this afternoon had told Selwyn, "No headlights, remember."

Two men got out of the ice cream van, and a

third climbed down from the cab of the cattle truck. Harrie watched in terrified fascination as the three men spoke to each other in low voices. A match flared as they lit cigarettes, and for an instant Harrie saw the gamekeeper's sallow face and the black strands of his hair. The small light died and another match was lit. "Never light three from the same match," said Selwyn. "Unlucky, see."

"Idiot," said the other man. "Brown, you help me get the hurdles out. And, Selwyn, cut that chain on the gate."

"It's the man with the posh voice!" hissed Harrie.

"Posh is the word," Ian muttered. "Worse than Neil."

Selwyn laughed with mock admiration and said, "Takes more than a bit of chain to keep our Gerald out." Then he added in a clumsy imitation of the other man's upper-class accent, "Good old Gerald, what?"

"That's enough!" snapped the man called Gerald angrily. "Get on with your job."

The gamekeeper slouched unwillingly back to the cattle truck and fished about in the cab, then hauled out a heavy metal tool. "Bolt cutter," muttered Ian. The other two men had opened the rear doors of the ice cream van and were dragging out some wooden sheep hurdles. Selwyn went to the field gate and there was a heavy, rattling clink as the padlock and chain fell to the ground, cut through by the bolt cutter.

Ian clutched his head in his hands. "What are we going to *do*?" he whispered desperately. "We can't flash the light—they'd be on us."

"And we can't get past them to fetch Dad," breathed Harrie. She was almost crying. "Oh, Ian—we *must* do something!"

The gate was open now, and the men let down the tailboard of the cattle truck. It had folding gates that fitted as sides to the ramp, and the men arranged the hurdles to block the gap between the ramp and the gateway, tying them in·place with lengths of bale string.

"Now, my little beauties," said the man called Gerald. "Where are you?" All three men stared across the field in the moonlight.

"Blast it," said Selwyn, "they're right down at the bottom. They would be, wouldn't they?"

"Not to panic," said Gerald calmly. "Who in their right mind would expect a job at this time of night? The local yokels will be swilling ale in the Pig and Whistle, and they won't get their stupid posse organized for ages yet. They still believe in the witching hour around here—nasty things always happen at midnight. Or so they hope!"

The third man spoke for the first time. "I sink ve

be quick, yes?" he said, in a thick foreign accent.

"Right," said Selwyn approvingly. "There's sense for you. Come on!"

They set off across the field.

Ian got to his feet cautiously. "Listen," he said quietly, "we've got a few minutes while they round the cattle up. There isn't time to go home—they'll have loaded them and gone before Dad could get back here. We *must* stop them getting away. If we cut the hurdles loose, we might be able to move the cattle truck. I think I could drive it—I've watched Dad often enough."

"But, Ian, you've never tried," said Harrie. "And what if we didn't manage it properly and they drove the cattle up to the gate and they all got out? They'd go crashing down the quarry the way you said, and that would be just as bad!"

"M'm," Ian admitted reluctantly. He stared across at the quarry fence. Then he grabbed Harrie by both arms. "Hey! That's brilliant! I know what we'll do!" He ran across to the ice cream van. "Come on!"

Harrie followed him. "Ian, what do you mean?" she asked.

Ian was already inside the van, whose rear doors had been left open. "I'm going to let the hand brake off," he said, "and then we'll push it over the edge."

"Down into the quarry?"

"Yes." Ian released the hand brake and hauled the steering wheel around so that the van would run toward the fence. "There," he said. "Oh— may as well see what they've got in these freezers. It won't be ice cream. Illegally slaughtered meat, I expect."

He pulled up the lid, and he and Harrie gazed down into the frosty container. It was not meat. It was a big, huddled shape, dark colored.

"It looks like old clothes," said Harrie, puzzled. "Open the other lid, Ian."

When Ian did so, she had to smother a scream. For the huddled shape ended in a shoulder and a collar and a stiff, white hand—and a large, round, pale object that gleamed in the moonlight like the top of a giant ice cream cone. Ian and Harrie looked at each other aghast and said in chorus, "The bald man." The discovery was so appalling that Harrie felt madly inclined to laugh. "He said Baldy was keeping cool," she remembered. "I see what he meant now."

Ian slammed down the lid. "Come on," he said. "They'll be back any minute."

Harrie put Mutty's lead down on the ground and said sternly, "*Stay*, Mutty." He sat down obediently and watched while Ian and Harrie shut the van's doors and began to push. It seemed impossi-

bly heavy. "It *must* go," said Ian through clenched teeth. Harrie threw all her weight against her hands and heaved desperately. The van rolled forward—and then slipped back again into the ruts it had made in the loose gravel. "Again!" panted Ian. Twice more it rolled back, and then, as Harrie felt as if her chest was going to burst with the effort, the van went forward and kept going. "Keep it up!" gasped Ian. The van gathered a little speed as it bumped over the smooth grass at the edge of the turnout, then there was a splintering crunch as it hit the fence—and stuck.

"Oh, *no!*" groaned Harrie. She and Ian rushed around to the front of the van and attacked the fence, pushing and kicking at it. "Want a hammer or something," gasped Ian. "Bolt cutter!" He dashed across to the cattle truck and snatched the heavy tool from the cab. Swinging it in both hands, he assaulted the fence like a maniac, careless of the noise as the wood shattered into fragments.

"That'll do," he said. "Push again."

They ran to the rear of the van and heaved with new desperation—and this time the result was amazingly easy. The van began to move and suddenly it was rolling of its own accord, away from them. In the next instant it had plunged out of sight, hurtling away down the quarry with a series of deafening crashes and clangs. The sudden noise was too much for Mutty. He turned and fled back toward the airfield, tripping and stumbling over his trailing lead as he went.

"No, *this* way, Mutty," shouted Harrie frantically. There was no point in trying to be quiet now. The cattle were coming up the field, the men shouting behind them.

"*Mutty!*"

"Blasted dog," said Ian, turning toward home. "Come on, Harrie. Leave him."

"I *can't*," said Harrie. "They might kill him. Mutty!"

And she rushed after him.

There was no time to argue. The men were almost at the gate. Ian hesitated for a moment, as if toying with the idea of going to fetch help. But he could not leave Harrie alone on the airfield. He heaved a sigh and ran after her.

There was a shout from behind them as the men saw that the van had gone, and in the next moment they had jumped over the hurdles and were in the lane. Ian and Harrie again fled into the prickly shelter of the blackberry bushes with Mutty as the men rushed to the yawning gap in the fence and stared down into the quarry.

"You bloody fool, you left the brake off!" shouted Selwyn.

"I did not," said Gerald positively. "And if I had, it wouldn't have gone that way. It's been steered down there. Look, the fence has been smashed."

"They're onto us, then!" said Selwyn frantically. "We'd best get out of here, quick!"

"I told you before, my dear chap, don't panic!" said Gerald. " 'They' didn't come in a car. No sign of a vehicle anywhere. So they're probably kids. You said you'd had a spot of trouble with some children, didn't you? Now, they can't be far away. Probably squatting under some bush, scared stiff. All we have to do is find them. Then we'll put them in the truck along with the cattle and presto—next stop Belgium."

"They'll shout," objected Selwyn.

"Not with broken necks they won't," said Gerald tightly. "Now, have a cigarette and calm down. Then we'll spread out and catch them."

Harrie felt for Ian's hand and clutched it. "Where's the light?" she breathed.

"I left it by the van," Ian whispered back. "Needed two hands to push with. Sorry."

"Oh, *no*!" Harrie was in despair. Their brave effort had failed and now they were marooned on the wrong side of the dreadful men. And they hadn't even got the means of signaling to Neil.

Ian squeezed her hand reassuringly. "It's all

right," he whispered. "We know this airfield better than they do. And they might walk right past us here—as long as that dog doesn't bark."

"He won't," promised Harrie.

The group of men by the quarry's edge lit cigarettes and Gerald said scornfully. "I suppose you want a match of your own, do you, Selwyn?"

"Yes, please," said the gamekeeper apologetically. "Only a superstition, I know, but—"

He got no further. As Gerald threw the still-burning match down contemptuously, a sheet of flame broke from his feet and blazed its way down into the quarry, following the trail of gasoline spilled from the ice cream van. In the next second there was a shattering explosion and the whole scene was lit up by the fire that burned at the bottom of the sheer drop.

Mutty jumped to his feet, the hair along his back bristling. He gave a long, deep growl, then burst into a frenzy of barking. There was nothing Harrie could do to stop him.

The three men leaped around, their faces a livid pink in the light of the flames.

"There they are!" shouted Selwyn. "That's them!"

Ian and Harrie were already away, running like hares across the broken concrete. Mutty, no longer barking, bounded along between them as fast as his lead would allow.

"Make for the buildings!" panted Ian. "Dodge around them. Try and shake them off."

They reached the first group of buildings and dived between them. Harrie thought Ian meant to shelter inside and ran in through a doorway with Mutty, then realized that Ian had gone on to the next building—or perhaps even further. Heavy footsteps approached. "There he is!" shouted Selwyn.

"Vere is ze ozzer? And ze dog?" asked the foreign man. They stopped, panting hard, just outside the wall of the building where Harrie cowered, clutching at Mutty's muzzle so that he should not give her away again by barking. Oh, if only she had taken Ian's advice and left the dog at home!

"Go for the boy first," decided Gerald. "We can make him tell us where the other one is."

They ran off again, and Harrie was alone in the ruined building. The floor was littered with rotten timber and half-bricks, and it smelled of cats. Harrie looked up at the moonlit sky through the jagged pattern of broken beams. Why had she ever found the airfield frightening on ordinary, everyday afternoons when nobody was chasing her? Compared with the fear she felt now, the previous sense of creepiness was nothing. Wind-blown clouds scudded past the moon as they must have done all those years ago when the airmen waited to be called out to their planes. For the first time, Harrie felt the unknown, long-departed men to be her friends. They, too, had been frightened. She was not alone. Mutty lay down at her feet and put his head on his paws.

Harrie listened intently, trying to make out what was going on. Where was Ian? What if the men had caught him? He would put up a fight, but a boy of twelve was no match for three grown men. Oh, please God, let him escape. Harrie stuffed her clenched fists into her pockets. Although she was still hot from running, she began to shiver. The silence hummed around her.

Suddenly, and horribly close at hand, there were footsteps. They approached the door. Someone was coming in. Harrie flattened herself against the wall.

"Harrie!" whispered Ian. "Are you there?"

"Ian!" She could have kissed him. "What's happening? Where are they?"

"I gave them the slip around the straw stacks," said Ian, panting. "Stayed on the grass—not so noisy as running on the concrete. Don't know where they are. Have you heard them come back?"

"No," whispered Harrie. "I think they're still looking for you."

When he had got his breath back a little, Ian said, "Perhaps we'd better make a run for home."

"What if they see us?" asked Harrie fearfully.

"Ssh!" Ian held up a hand. "They're coming."

The heavy footsteps approached again, slower now, half running and half walking.

"I sink ve go," said the foreign man.

"So do I," agreed Selwyn. "It was silly going after those kids. They'll be home and dry by now, telling the tale to their parents. Let's put the truck back where it came from and leave it at that."

"Not on your life," said Gerald. For the first time, he sounded rattled. "If we put the truck back, we've got no transport. All right for you, Selwyn—you live here. Brown and I have got to get out and the van's down the quarry. We've *got* to have the cattle truck. Now, come *on!*"

"Thought you said don't panic," muttered Selwyn. Then they all set off.

Ian and Harrie heaved sighs of relief. "Close shave," murmured Ian.

Harrie had been so frightened on her brother's behalf that she had forgotten to be scared for herself. "We can't just let them go, Ian," she urged. "Not after all this. Come on—let's see what they're doing. There might still be some way of stopping them."

Ian laughed. "Good old Harrie!" he said. "All right—but be careful. It's not exactly safe out there, you know."

"Oh, yes," said Harrie, nodding. "I *do* know."

And, very cautiously, they left the shelter of the building and went out across the moonlit airfield.

Chapter 8
Mutty Helps

As they neared the quarry lane, Ian and Harrie crept carefully from one patch of shelter to another, taking care not to be seen. They scurried from bush to tree to clump of gorse as quietly as they could, bending low so that they would not be noticed by a casual glance. Mutty trotted meekly at Harrie's heels. He was beginning to look a little weary after his unusually long evening walk, Harrie thought. But as the wind brought the reek of fire from the quarry to his nose the dog growled softly, and when they crouched in the shelter of a blackberry thicket Harrie could feel the hair on his back standing up, and she knew that he was still suspicious and uneasy.

The men had obviously abandoned their plan to take the cattle. They were bundling the hurdles into the back of the cattle truck, and when they had finished they folded the side gates in and pushed the ramp up, where it locked with a clang. Selwyn was trying to wind the broken chain around the field gate to hold it shut.

"Don't fiddle about with that, Selwyn," said Gerald irritably. "Never mind the blasted cattle— let's get out of here."

"Go on, then," said Selwyn flatly. "I'm not stopping you."

"But you've got to come with us," Gerald insisted. "I'll need you to bring the truck back. And we must make a plan—decide what to do."

"You're the one as does the planning," said Selwyn sulkily. "I'm going home."

Gerald glared at him. "You'll regret this!" he shouted. Then he climbed into the driver's seat of the cattle truck and started the engine. The foreign man climbed in beside him.

"They're *going*," said Harrie despairingly.

"But they haven't taken the cattle," said Ian. "That's the main thing."

The truck began to move. It pulled away from the gate, across into the turnout, where it just had room to turn down into the lane.

"They'll go all the way along the lane to the main road," said Ian. "And that'll be that."

They watched gloomily as the cattle truck entered the dark part of the lane, where the hedges screened off the glare of the fire. Its headlights beamed out, lighting up the narrow lane. Obviously, Harrie thought, there was no need for secrecy now. They were all for a quick getaway. Then she gasped.

Around the corner of the lane, caught in the truck's headlights like a fly in the flashlight beam, came a small, tubby figure, arms held out in a pathetic effort to stop the huge vehicle that was bearing down on him.

"It's Neil!" shrieked Harrie. "Neil! Be careful!"

Ian had already leaped to his feet and was rushing after the cattle truck. Harrie was so horrified by the conviction that Neil was going to be mowed down that her legs seemed to turn to water. She stared, hypnotized. If it had not been so dreadful, Neil would have looked comic. He was out of breath from running, his face screwed up with fear and determination and his eyes tightly shut behind their round glasses so that he would not see the thing that was about to kill him. And he still held out his arms in the brave, futile gesture of defiance.

The cattle truck slowed down.

"Get out of the way!" Harrie heard Gerald

shout. "You stupid little—" The cattle truck slowed down to walking pace although it was still advancing on Neil. Then Ian caught up with it. He leaped onto the step behind the front wheel, opened the door, and slammed the kill button, which switched off the diesel engine. Gerald hurled Ian out of the way as he jumped out of the cab, and Harrie saw the other door open as the foreign man got out as well.

Suddenly released from the horrified spell that had bound her, Harrie found the use of her legs and rushed along the lane toward the truck. As she passed the gate to the cattle field, a dark figure stepped from the hedge and caught her across the shoulders in a strong grip.

"Oh, no, you don't," snarled the gamekeeper. "You've caused enough trouble, you have."

Harrie screamed. And Mutty, with a savage, rattling growl that Harrie had never heard him utter before, sank his teeth into the man's leg. Selwyn gave a yell and let go of Harrie so that he could turn to face the dog. Mutty hung on grimly, still growling. The gamekeeper aimed a blow at him, but lost his balance and fell heavily. Mutty released his grip but stood over the man, snarling steadily and snapping at his face fiercely every time the gamekeeper tried to get up. A big dog at the best of times, he looked twice the size with the fur on his neck and back raised in a bristling ridge.

"Stay there, Mutty," said Harrie. "Stay with him."

Glancing back at the dog to see that he was not going to let the gamekeeper go, she ran on down to the truck, where Ian and Neil were struggling in the lane with the two men.

Gerald flung Ian aside into the hedge and swung himself up into the cab—but Ian had picked himself up and was after the man again like a terrier, hauling at his leg to try and drag him out. Harrie joined in, grabbing Gerald's other foot and heaving as hard as she could. He kicked out hard, sending Harrie staggering backward and leaving his shoe clutched uselessly in her hands. He started the engine and as it roared into life, kicked savagely again to release Ian's hold on his other leg. The kick caught Ian on the side of the face, and Harrie saw her brother clap his hand to his eye as he fell back on to the grass.

The truck started to move. Where was Neil? Harrie dashed around the back of the vehicle and saw the foreign man grab at the handle of the passenger door to get in. She flung herself at him recklessly, but at that moment the truck stopped momentarily and the opening edge of the door knocked her flying.

"Ze boy is dead, I sink," said the foreign man as he got into the cattle truck.

"Never mind!" snapped Gerald.

By the time the door slammed shut, the truck was moving fast down the lane.

Harrie lay face down on the grass where she had landed, gasping for breath. She felt dizzy and rather sick, and she seemed to hurt all over, especially her left elbow. The rustlers had escaped after all, she thought dismally. And *what* had happened to Neil?

Then she heard the truck stop. Doors slammed and there was a confusion of men's voices, shouting. Painfully, Harrie rolled over and sat up, holding her elbow. There were lights shining at the end of the lane. More than that—a blue light was flashing on and off. The police must have arrived.

"Harrie," said an anxious voice quite near her, "are you all right?"

"*Neil!* Oh, thank goodness—I thought you were dead!"

"I pretended I was," Neil admitted, squatting down beside Harrie on the grass. "That foreign chap was so strong, I felt as if I were made of paper. So I just went limp and pretended I was dead, before I really was! That's the trouble with being a coward, you see," he added sheepishly.

"You're *not* a coward," said Harrie. "Stopping

that cattle truck in the lane was the bravest thing I've ever seen. Where's Ian? Have you seen him?"

"No," said Neil. "I thought he was with you."

Harrie struggled to her feet, still feeling very shaky. "Ian!" she called. "Where are you?"

There was no reply.

"What have you done to your arm?" asked Neil.

"I think I fell on a stone or something," said Harrie. "My fingers have gone all tingly. Ian!" she called again.

"Perhaps it's your funny bone," said Neil.

Ian came running up the lane toward them. "The police have got the two men!" he said excitedly. "There was a terrific fight—it was marvelous! They put handcuffs on them and shoved them in the van. And Gerald's only got one shoe on—he looks ever so funny."

"The other one's here," said Harrie, pointing at the grass beside her. "It came off when we were trying to pull him out."

"Your mum and dad turned up as well," Ian said to Neil. "Your mum's a bit frantic."

"Oh, dear," said Neil guiltily. "Yes, I expect she is."

Just then, Harrie heard Mutty yelp.

"Mutty!" she gasped. "Oh, Heavens—we've been ages. I do hope he's all right."

Forgetting her bruises, she set off up the lane as fast as she could go.

"Where is he?" asked Ian, following at her heels.

"By the gate," Harrie told him over her shoulder. "He's got the gamekeeper. Oh, do hurry— that beastly man may have killed him!"

Chapter 9
Stampede!

The gamekeeper was on his feet but had his back to the gate, kicking out at Mutty, who stood menacingly in front of him, still growling. Blood dripped from a cut on the dog's lip where a kick had connected.

"Call this blasted dog off!" the man shouted when he saw Harrie coming, with Ian and Neil close behind her. "And you'd best get him put down pretty quick or I'll shoot him myself next time I see him. He'd be dead now if I'd had my gun with me."

"You're not going to shoot *anything*," said Ian furiously. "Not ever again. I hope they put you in prison for ever and ever."

Clearly lit here by the red glow of the fire in the quarry, Harrie could see that her brother's eye was bruised and swollen. "Oh, Ian," she said, "you're going to have an awful black eye."

"His beastly friend kicked me, didn't he," said Ian, nodding at the gamekeeper. "They're good at kicking things. Look at Mutty's lip."

The gamekeeper glanced at the dog, then at the children. Then he smiled ingratiatingly and said in a different kind of voice altogether, "Now, let's not make any mistakes. I'm only here to do my job, so don't mix me up with anyone else you may have seen tonight."

The children stared at him in disbelief.

"Yes, I thought I'd better make sure the cattle were safe," the man went on, "seeing as there's all this talk of rustlers. Just as well I did, too, for someone's been interfering with this gate. They cut the chain clean through, see? Look at this here." And he held up the severed chain.

Harrie opened her mouth to protest but cries of, "Neil! Where are you?" came from the lane and interrupted what she was going to say. Two figures hurried toward them.

"Neil! Is that you?"

"Hello, Mum," said Neil.

"Why on earth did you go off like that?" demanded Mrs. Grey. "You could have *said*. We were worried sick."

"I wasn't *meaning* to go," said Neil. "I just went into the garden to get a better look at the fire, after I'd seen it from the bedroom and told you. Then I felt awful, knowing Ian and Harrie were up here—I thought they might be in real danger or something. And I knew you'd come as soon as you'd finished ringing up the police and the fire department. So I just came on ahead to see if there was anything I could do."

"Never thought he had it in him," said Neil's father proudly.

"Thank goodness you did come, Neil," said Harrie. "If it hadn't been for you, they'd have got clean away."

Mr. Grey was staring doubtfully at the gamekeeper, who was edging along the gate, still keeping a wary eye on Mutty. "Who's your friend?" he asked.

"He isn't a friend," said Neil.

"He's one of the rustlers," Harrie told them. "He grabbed me when I was coming down the lane, after Neil had stopped the cattle truck—but Mutty bit him."

"We'd better take him down to the police," said Ian.

"They're mostly down in the quarry," said Neil's father. "We phoned the fire department, but they're not here yet. I suppose the police think they've got the whole gang."

The gamekeeper spoke directly to Mrs. Grey, who was looking very confused. "You seem like a sensible lady, madam," he said. "Now, I'm sure you'll understand. These kiddies got it all wrong, see. I had nothing to do with all this. I just came out when I heard the bang and saw the fire. Thought I'd best see what was going on, like. I'm in charge of the shooting estate here, you see. On the side of law and order, I am."

"Oh!" Mrs. Grey smiled and held out her hand. "How do you do?"

The children all shouted their protests together at this absurd pretense, and Ian said, "We saw you get out of the cattle truck. And we saw you cut the chain on the gate. You'd never have come out here without your gun if you'd come to see what was happening—but you needed both hands free, didn't you!"

"And anyway," put in Harrie, "I was in the building where the cattle truck was hidden, and I heard you talking to that man called Gerald. That rustle you thought was a rat—that was me and Mutty."

"Don't let him fool you," Ian said to Mrs. Grey. "We know all about it."

"I'll nip down and get the police," said Mr. Grey.

"Don't be silly," said the gamekeeper desperately. "It's all a mistake." He had sidled along the gate until he reached its opening edge, and before anyone had realized what he was going to do, he pulled off the loose chain, slipped through the gap, and ran off across the field between the startled bullocks.

"Come on!" shouted Ian, dashing through the gate after him. "He mustn't get away now!"

Neil was at his heels, followed by Mr. Grey. Harrie and Mutty set off after them, but Mrs. Grey stayed where she was by the gate and Harrie heard her saying, "Are you sure, dear? He seems such a nice man. . . ."

"Get the police!" Harrie shouted back.

She ran awkwardly, her elbow hurting at every jogging footstep. The boys and Mr. Grey were well ahead. In a few minutes more she slowed to a walk, and Mutty willingly slackened his pace so that he ambled beside her, his head drooping. Harrie knew he was tired. At this time of night he expected to be curled up in front of the stove in the kitchen.

There was no point in trying to catch up with the boys. Harrie plodded steadily across the dark field, nursing her elbow in the other hand. Then she heard shouts ahead of her. Ian's voice came clearly—"Oh, great! What a beauty!" It sounded as if they had caught the gamekeeper. Harrie gave a small sigh of relief. Just as well she hadn't bothered to slog all the way down there. Mr. Grey was a strong-looking man even if he was a bit fat, and with Ian and Neil to help, they should be able to manage all right.

The cattle, disturbed afresh by this new excitement, began to thunder across the field from the far end where the boys were. A terrible thought struck Harrie. The gate! If Mrs. Grey had gone to get the police, she would never have thought of securing the gate behind her. There was nothing to stop the cattle from charging through the open gateway and down into the quarry.

Desperately, all pain forgotten, Harrie began to run headlong back up the field, trying to get to the gate before the cattle—but they overtook her easily, bucking and kicking up their heels as they galloped past, heading with suicidal determination toward the open gate.

"Oh, Mutty!" cried Harrie, "what can we *do*?" She stumbled on and then trod in a cowpat and her foot slid from under her. She fell headlong, struggled up again, and went on, dirty and bedraggled and hopeless. It was no good. The cattle were miles ahead, a confused mass of black and white, almost at the gate now.

Harrie began to cry.

A man's voice shouted from the gate, "Stop! Stay where you are, all of you!"

What a funny way to talk to cattle, Harrie thought idiotically, rubbing her sleeve across her face because she hadn't got a hanky. But at least somebody was there. Thank heavens.

And then her father's voice shouted, "We are armed. We will shoot if necessary. Come forward with your hands up."

Suddenly Harrie understood. It was the farmers' patrol. And they thought someone in the field was after the cattle.

"Dad!" she screamed. "It's me! Harrie! Don't shoot!"

Flashlights and headlights beamed out from the gate, which, Harrie saw with relief, was blocked by men and vehicles. The cattle turned abruptly in the sudden light, swerved across the top of the field, and began to run back toward Harrie. Heading into the dark as they were, she thought for a hideous moment that they were going to trample straight over her, not even knowing she was there. But Mutty charged at the galloping bullocks, barking and snapping so fiercely that they changed direction to avoid him and veered past, narrowly missing Harrie. Clods of mud thrown up by their thundering hooves spattered her and the dog, but they were safe.

Mr. Armstrong came running across the grass with his shotgun in one hand, Andrew Corrie at his heels carrying a rifle.

"Harrie!" he said, hugging his daughter, "are you all right?—here, Andrew, hold this gun a minute—Harrie, what are you doing here? Why is the gate open?"

"They cut the chain," said Harrie—but before she could explain any further, several more people arrived, her mother among them.

"Oh, Harrie!" she said. "*There* you are! We called in at home for the flashlight and found you'd taken it and not come back—where's Ian? What's happening?"

"How did that fire start in the quarry?" asked Andrew. "It's a hell of a blaze?"

"The police are here," said Harrie, confused by all the questions. "Didn't you see them?"

"Down the lane, d'you mean?" asked her father. "We saw a flashing light as we came across the airfield, but we thought that was the fire department."

"The fire department *is* here," reported another farmer who had just joined the group. "They say it's nearly under control. There's a cattle truck along there with the police—something about rustlers. They seem to have caught a gang, but they're too busy nattering into their walkie-talkies to tell me what's happened."

"I think Harrie knows," said Mr. Armstrong. "Harrie, what on earth is going on?"

Harrie took a deep breath. "Some men tried to rustle our cattle," she said. "The men we told you about. And the gamekeeper is one of them, but he got away and Ian chased him with Neil and his father. I think they caught him—they're down the field, there." She pointed with her good arm. "And the police have got the other two."

"Come on, Bill," said Andrew Corrie, starting down the field. "Those lads may need help."

"Coming," said Mr. Armstrong. "Now, Harrie, stay with Mum. I'll be back in a minute."

Harrie walked back toward the gate, holding her mother's hand tightly. Her other arm hurt a lot when it was straight, but it felt better if she held it across her chest.

"I still can't see what you were doing here," said her mother anxiously. "You promised me you'd be home by dark."

Harrie nodded speechlessly. Tears began to trickle down her face. Her mother bent and kissed her. "There, pet, don't cry," she said. "I'm not cross—I was just a bit worried, that's all. Why are you holding your arm like that? Have you hurt it?"

Harrie nodded, gulping, and said, "I think I fell on a stone."

"We'll have a look at that as soon as we get home," said her mother. "You might have broken it."

The police were waiting at the gate. Two police cars had come up the lane and stood with their roof lights flashing, and although the strong smell of burning still drifted from the quarry, the red glow had gone.

Mrs. Grey was peering anxiously into the darkness. "Where's Neil?" she asked when she saw Harrie. "What's happened?"

"He's just coming," said Harrie. "I think they've got the man."

Two policemen set off across the field on hearing this, but in a few moments Harrie saw their powerful flashlights illumine the little group coming toward them. The gamekeeper stumbled along between Mr. Armstrong and Andrew Corrie, who held him firmly by an arm each. Neil's father, very muddy but beaming broadly, carried Mr. Armstrong's gun and Andrew's rifle, and Ian and Neil walked proudly alongside.

"You should have seen Mr. Grey's football tackle!" shouted Ian as they approached. "Fantastic!"

"And I sat on him," said Neil, grinning.

"Oh, yes!" agreed his father. "That finished him!"

Selwyn's face was grazed and muddy. As his hands were pinioned by his captors, he jerked his head to try and flick the greasy strands of black hair away from his eyes.

"Now, wait a minute," he said as a policeman snapped handcuffs onto his wrists. "There's something I got to tell you."

Ian groaned and said, "Not again!"

"No, this is something different," the game-keeper went on. "It's about Mr. Ashworth. I rang up his club in London, see. Tried to tip him off, like. I told him his cattle were going to be pinched tonight—well, that is, I left a message. I didn't want to talk to him man to man, like, or he might have known who it was."

"And why shouldn't he?" inquired Mr. Armstrong coldly. "If you were so innocent you wouldn't mind giving your name."

"Ah, but he might not believe it," said Selwyn evasively. "He might have lumped me in with the others. But what I thought was, when he got the message he'd come back here right away, see, and then I'd have a good excuse for stopping the others going ahead with it."

"You never wanted to stop the others before," Harrie put in hotly. "I heard you this afternoon. So long as you got paid, you said, you didn't care."

"I don't believe a word of it, anyway," said Andrew Corrie. "How would *you* know what club he belongs to? I've been running his farm for him for eleven years, and *I* don't know."

"Gerald does," said Selwyn simply. "He's a fellow member."

A fireman arrived, his face black with smoke.

"The fire's well out now," he reported. "But we'll go on damping down for a bit, just to make sure."

"What caused it?" asked a policeman.

"Can't say for certain yet," said the fireman. "There's a burned-out van down there—children could have been playing with matches, possibly, set the gas alight. But, of course, that kind of explosion will cause severe injury to anyone nearby—and there's no sign of anybody."

"We pushed the van over," Harrie told him. "Down into the quarry. It was the only way to—"

"*Did* you?" interrupted Neil, who had not heard about this part of the night's activities. "Gosh, how terrific!"

"And there's a body in the freezer," Ian joined

in. "It's the man we found in the wood—the bald man. I *told* you he was dead!"

"*No!*" said Neil.

"Good God," said Mr. Armstrong.

Mrs. Grey looked very puzzled and said, "What freezer? I don't understand."

"It was an ice cream van," explained Harrie.

The fireman waited for no more but turned and ran back in the direction of the quarry. They heard his voice in the distance, shouting, "Hose that van down—get it cooled off so we can get inside!" Several policemen followed him.

Selwyn was looking at Harrie and Ian, aghast. "You found Baldy?" he asked. "In the wood?"

"Of course we did," said Ian contemptuously. "That's why we were looking at the tire tracks. We knew someone had come to take him away—and not in a Mini van, either."

"There's a thing," said Selwyn regretfully, shaking his head. "I'd never have wanted that to happen. And to think of him being in the freezer, right under my nose. 'Keeping cool,' he said. I see what he meant now!"

A policeman came over with something in his hand.

"Does this object belong to any of you gentlemen?" he inquired. In the flashing lights Harrie could see that he was holding the bolt cutter that

Ian had dropped on the grass when they pushed the van over.

Andrew Corrie shook his head. "Not the farm one," he said. "Ours has got red-painted handles. Yours, Bill?"

"Nothing to do with me," said Mr. Armstrong.

Ian nodded at the gamekeeper and said, "He used it to cut the chain on the gate. We saw him. He took it out of the cattle truck—behind the driver's seat."

"Right," said the policeman. "We'll keep this."

Ian remembered something and darted across to the quarry's edge.

"Do be careful, dear!" called Mrs. Grey. "You don't want to slip over!"

Harrie smiled to herself. It was a good thing Mrs. Grey had not seen what they had been up to this evening!

"Here it is," said Ian, switching on his father's flashlight, which he had found in the grass. "Look, it still works OK."

He swung the long beam down the lane—and illuminated the tall figure of a man in a tweed suit walking toward them.

"It's Mr. Ashworth!" exclaimed Harrie.

"There you are!" said Selwyn triumphantly. "That proves it! I told you I sent him a message— now you can see I wanted nothing to do with all this! Good evening, sir!" he added as Mr. Ashworth approached. "I'm glad you got here!"

Mr. Ashworth stared at him without speaking. Then he said to the policemen, "Take him away."

Despite everything, Harrie felt almost sorry for the protesting Selwyn as two policemen escorted him down the lane toward a large police van that stood waiting.

"Well, Andrew—and you, Bill—it seems I have a lot to thank you for," said Mr. Ashworth. "I don't know the details yet, but I gather that your patrol has stopped these wretched people just in time."

"It wasn't us, sir," said Andrew Corrie. "It was these three children. I haven't found out quite what it was they did, but whatever it was, it worked. They had the whole gang tied in knots before we ever got here."

"*Really?*" Mr. Ashworth was impressed. He bent down and peered more closely at the children's faces in the flickering light of the police-car lights. "Oh, yes!" he said, recognizing them. "You two are Armstrongs, aren't you? And who's this?"

"Neil Grey," said Neil.

"He's only just come to live here," explained Harrie.

Still talking, they all started down the lane toward the police van. Dozens of other vehicles seemed to have arrived as well; there were two fire engines, the Greys' car, several police cars and a fire department car. Nearly all the vehicles had blue or red lights flashing, and as Harrie and the others approached, an ambulance came slowly up the lane, its red light adding yet another note of color to the garish scene.

Harrie looked at the ambulance with some anxiety and asked, "Is anyone hurt?"

"Baldy is," said Ian grimly.

"Oh. Yes, of course." Harrie felt slightly embarrassed. The thought of the bald man crammed into the freezer in the ice cream van still made her quake with a kind of horrified laughter.

Mr. Ashworth, who had been quiet for some time, shook his head with admiration. "I can't tell you how grateful I am," he said. "Not just for myself, you know, but for all the other farmers whose stock would have been taken if these people hadn't been stopped. Who are they, do you know?"

"The gamekeeper is one," said Ian. "Mr. Selwyn."

"I know," said Mr. Ashworth. "I smelled a rat when the steward told me there'd been a telephone message from a man with a Welsh accent who wouldn't give his name. Nasty piece of work. He was recommended by a friend of mine at the club, but I've never been sure I picked the right man."

He stumbled slightly, tripping over a loose object in the lane, then stopped and picked the thing up. "It's a man's shoe," he said, puzzled. "How odd. But you were telling me about these men. Who are the others?"

"One's a Belgian," said Harrie. "I think they call him Brown. And that shoe belongs to—"

But Mr. Ashworth's attention was distracted from what Harrie was saying as the policemen opened the rear doors of the van. A harsh white light glared from the bulb in the ceiling of the van, showing up the two men who sat there with their wrists in handcuffs as clearly as if they had been actors on a floodlit stage. Until now, Harrie had only seen them in the dark, and she watched in fascination as the fair-haired Gerald glanced up as casually as a man recognizing an acquaintance in a crowd.

"Ah, Peter," he said as he spotted Mr. Ashworth, "you've brought my shoe. Decent of you."

"*Gerald!*" Mr. Ashworth stared at his friend, thunderstruck. "What on earth are *you* doing here?" Then he looked at the mud on Gerald's

face, at his torn shirt-sleeve and at the gleaming steel handcuffs. As the truth became obvious, his face crumpled with disgust. "Oh, no," he said.

"Game's up, I'm afraid, old chap," said Gerald. "Rumbled. By a couple of snotties, too."

Harrie felt Ian clench his fists.

"Don't you speak about my friends like that!" snapped Mr. Ashworth. "It's a good thing some people are honest!"

"Honest?" Gerald smiled tiredly. "Do you know what the word means, old boy? You live on the proceeds of other people's work. So do I—but at least I get my hands dirty." He displayed his handcuffed hands, which, Harrie thought, didn't look very dirty at all. But then she remembered what her father had said about sheep being killed in the field, and she knew that Gerald's hands must have been red with blood to the elbow, killing and skinning and gutting. And she felt sick.

The policemen bundled Selwyn into the van, where he sat scowling, as far away from the other two as he could. With a dismissive gesture of disgust, Mr. Ashworth tossed Gerald's shoe into the van and turned away as the doors were slammed shut.

"No wonder Gerald recommended Selwyn," he said bitterly. "I can see it all now. What a fool I've been."

A policeman coughed politely and said, "If you ladies and gentlemen will follow us back to the station, we'll take statements there."

"Sorry," said Mrs. Armstrong promptly, "but these children have got to go home. Harrie's hurt her arm, and Ian's got an awful black eye, and it's time they were both in bed. It'll keep until tomorrow, won't it?"

"Well," said the policeman reluctantly, "if you insist, madam."

"Time Neil was in bed, too," agreed Mrs. Grey.

"Time *I* was!" put in Mr. Grey, grinning. "I haven't had such a strenuous day since I gave up playing football."

"Can we go around to Ian and Harrie's tomorrow?" asked Neil. "Then the police can see us all together if they want to. And, anyway, I've thought of lots of things I want to ask Mr. Armstrong about model airplanes!"

Harrie groaned, but the policeman seemed to think this was quite a good idea. The two fire engines drove away, followed by the fire department car, the police van, and a police car. As their lights disappeared down the lane, it suddenly seemed very cold and dark.

"Come on," said Mr. Armstrong. "Home."

The Land Rover was still standing by the field gate with the other farmers' vehicles. Mutty plodded wearily beside Harrie as they walked back up the dark lane, and when they reached the Land Rover he climbed into the front seat after her, put his big head on her lap, and at once went to sleep.

"Move over, Mutty," said Mrs. Armstrong, getting in as well. "You ought to be in the back, really."

"Good old Mutty," said Harrie, stroking the dog's shaggy ears. "I almost wished I'd left him at home, but then he saved me from the gamekeeper—and he sent the cattle off when they nearly ran over me. I do hope his mouth is all right—that horrible man kicked him."

"We'll look at it when we get home," said her mother. "How is your arm?"

"All right if I keep it like this," said Harrie. She was beginning to feel beautifully warm and comfortable.

A blast of cold air came in briefly as Ian climbed into the back of the Land Rover. "Dad's just making sure the gate's secure," he reported. "Those men left bits of bale string all *over* the place."

A few minutes later Mr. Armstrong got into the driver's seat, laid his shotgun carefully in the back beside Ian, and started the engine.

"Well!" he said, as the headlights once again threw the lane and the hedges into bright relief, "what an evening!"

"It was great," said Ian with relish. "I wouldn't have missed it for anything. Would you, Harrie?"

But Harrie made no reply. She was fast asleep.

Chapter 10
The Morning After

On Monday morning Neil was waiting for them as Ian and Harrie came along the quarry lane. He grinned, and they grinned back. After so much talking yesterday, there didn't seem to be much to say.

It was a clear, fresh morning, too nice, Harrie thought, to be going to school. Mutty trotted ahead of them, his tail waving happily. When he reached the wire netting that had been fixed across the gap in the wooden fence above the quarry he stopped and sniffed carefully at it, then looked back at the children.

"It's all right, Mutty!" said Harrie. "We're not doing anything funny this morning!"

"Is he all right?" asked Neil. "That kick on his mouth didn't get infected or anything?"

"He's fine," said Harrie.

As if reassured, the dog trotted on, but he circled and came back when the three children stopped to stare down into the blackened depths of the quarry. The ice cream van had been towed out, but it would be a long time before the charred stubble of the trees and bushes grew again. One of the huts had been completely gutted, and a fire department car stood at the edge of the devastation, its driver talking to the quarry foreman and making notes on a clipboard.

"I wish I'd seen the ice cream van go down there," said Neil regretfully. "It must have been fantastic."

"You didn't miss anything," Harrie assured him. "It was so dark, we couldn't see a thing."

"But it blew up," said Neil.

"Not when we pushed it over," Ian insisted. "Gerald blew it up when he threw a match down and lit the gas that had spilled out."

"I'm glad it wasn't us," said Harrie, staring thoughtfully at the devastated quarry. "It's only luck that it wasn't, but I'd hate to think we caused all this."

"We did in a way," said Ian. "If we hadn't pushed the van over, the fire couldn't have started." He went on staring at the quarry for a minute, then added, "I wonder what sort of state old Baldy was in?"

"They wouldn't say, would they?" agreed Neil. "The policeman just said he was 'quite recognizable'."

"Mum says when you put a frozen roast in the oven, it takes quite a long time for it to thaw right through," said Harrie carefully. "That's why she gets it out of the freezer the day before. If you see what I mean."

The boys nodded. Then Ian said gleefully, "Bet he was a bit cooked, though!"

"No," insisted Harrie, "it's like that thing called a baked Alaska, when you have hot chocolate sauce around a frozen ice cream block. And, anyway, don't be so horrible! I think your black eye has brought out the worst in you!"

"You can talk," retorted Ian. "Standing there with your arm in a sling! Fancy having a chipped bone in your elbow!"

Harrie made a face at him and they walked on.

"That chap from the paper said they'd have a photographer at school this morning," Neil reminded them. "Miss Kemble will be furious!"

"No, she won't," said Ian. "She'll be wearing her best dress and smiling."

"You'd have thought they took enough photos yesterday," said Harrie. "They were at it all day. You and Dad and the airplanes, and Ian with the cattle, then me and Mutty, and all of us at the quarry, and Mr. Ashworth giving us those checks—"

"Wasn't that terrific!" interrupted Neil. "Fifty pounds each! I still can't get over it. I think I'll buy a radio control. What are you going to get, Ian?"

"I might buy a pig," said Ian. "Dad said I could run a few pigs if I could save up and buy the first one. I was going to rear a weaner, but now I might be able to buy an older one if I—"

"What about you, Harrie?" asked Neil, who was not interested in pigs.

"I don't know," said Harrie. "Mum said put it in the bank and forget about it. One day when I do know what I want, it'll be there, waiting."

"Well, I think the whole thing's terrific!" said Ian. "What a weekend! Talk about exciting!" He began to jump up and down, bursting with energy. "Come on, Neil—race you across the airfield!"

Neil, with no hope of catching him, set off good-naturedly in Ian's wake.

Harrie followed Mutty as he made his way from building to ruined building, stopping occasionally to sniff at a wall and cock his leg to mark the place with his own scent. In his way, Harrie thought, he was setting everything to rights again.

She stopped at the entrance to the roofless building that had sheltered her in those desperate moments on Saturday night. The wall felt cold in the sunshine after the autumn night. Harrie went inside and again looked up through the jagged rafters to the sky, which this morning was a pale, clear blue. An airplane, so high up that it was no more than a dot, traced a line of silver. And all around her again she could imagine the ghosts of the lost airmen, friendly now, and warm and laughing. The ruined building smelled of cats, and it didn't seem important to be there anymore. She would never be afraid of the airfield again.

Out in the sunshine, Harrie called, "Come on, Mutty!" But he was ahead of her, looking over his shoulder with cheerfully waving tail and lolling tongue, glad to be back in the old routine. She ran across the rest of the airfield and down the old road where the boys were waiting. There was no point in being late for school.

ABOUT THE AUTHOR

Alison Prince studied to be an artist at the Slade School and Goldsmith's College in England. She first earned her living as a teacher, occasionally selling paintings and etchings. After her marriage and the birth of three children, she turned to writing. She has contributed articles to the *Times Educational Supplement,* and she has also written several books for children, including *The Doubting Kind,* published in the United States in 1977, and *The Turkey's Nest,* published here in 1980.

ABOUT THE ILLUSTRATOR

Born in New Brunswick, New Jersey, Ellen Thompson received her B.F.A. from the Parsons School of Design in New York City. She is a freelance illustrator, and her work has appeared in various magazines, including the *New York Times Book Review, Seventeen,* and *Ms.* She lives in Somerset, New Jersey.